Solar Power

by Jim Ollhoff

VISIT US AT
WWW.ABDOPUBLISHING.COM

Published by ABDO Publishing Company, 8000 West 78th Street, Suite 310, Edina, MN 55439. Copyright ©2010 by Abdo Consulting Group, Inc. International copyrights reserved in all countries. No part of this book may be reproduced in any form without written permission from the publisher. ABDO & Daughters™ is a trademark and logo of ABDO Publishing Company.

Printed in the United States of America, North Mankato, Minnesota
112009
012010

 PRINTED ON RECYCLED PAPER

Editor: John Hamilton
Graphic Design: John Hamilton
Cover Photos: Jupiter Images, iStockphoto
Interior Photo: Corbis, p. 7; Getty Images, p. 5, 6, 11, 18, 19, 22, 23, 27, 28, 29; iStockphoto, p. 1, 15, 16, 17, 25; John Hamilton, p. 12; NASA, p. 13, 21; Photo Researchers, p. 9, 10, 14.

Library of Congress Cataloging-in-Publication Data

Ollhoff, Jim, 1959-
  Solar power / Jim Ollhoff.
    p. cm. -- (Future energy)
  Includes index.
  ISBN 978-1-60453-938-7
  1. Solar energy--Juvenile literature. I. Title.
  TJ810.3.O43 2010
  333.792'3--dc22
                    2009029933

Contents

Solar Power

Facing page: In this photo illustration, the earth floats above a set of solar panels. As a nonpolluting, renewable resource, solar power may someday provide a large part of our electrical needs.

Like a monster that eats everything in sight, we are consuming more and more electricity. North America's need for electricity increases daily. Our taste for oil, coal, and natural gas grows in leaps and bounds. These fossil fuels give us electricity, but they also give us things we don't want: pollution, climate change because of carbon dioxide and other greenhouse gasses, and a damaged environment.

However, there is an energy source that gives us electricity without pollution or environmental damage: the sun. If we could harness all the sun's energy that falls on the earth, solar power could provide 100 percent of the world's electrical needs. Unfortunately, right now we can only capture a fraction of the sun's energy. Night, cloudy days, and inefficient solar collectors reduce the amount of sunlight that can be turned into energy.

Solar power is a huge potential source of power. So far, it is virtually untapped in North America. It won't provide 100 percent of our electricity needs in the foreseeable future, but it could provide a large part. The job of harnessing solar power is a rapidly growing industry, and technological developments are beginning to come at a dizzying pace. Hopefully, with continued development, solar energy will help to power our future.

History of Solar Power

Solar energy has been used since ancient times. A chimney is a simple way to use solar power. The sun's heat warms up the chimney, which warms the air inside it. The warm air rises and exits the top of the chimney. Air from the outside then enters the home, providing a gentle breeze.

When sunlight is turned directly into electricity, it is called a *photoelectric* or *photovoltaic* effect. A French scientist, Alexandre-Edmond Becquerel, discovered the photoelectric effect in 1839. He noticed that certain materials could make a spark when struck with sunlight. The first working photovoltaic solar cell was created in the 1950s.

Left: French scientist Alexandre-Edmond Becquerel, who discovered the photoelectric effect in 1839.

During the late 1970s, there was an "energy crisis" caused by high oil prices from instability in the Middle East. There was a severe shortage of gasoline. Americans suddenly became fearful of having become so dependent on foreign oil. President Jimmy Carter funded many solar power projects, and even installed solar energy panels on the White House. Later presidents slashed solar power funding. By the early 1980s, the energy crisis was over. Oil and coal were cheap again, so people forgot about solar power. The urgency to research and implement solar power simply faded away.

Below: President Jimmy Carter giving a presentation in 1979 about newly installed solar panels at the White House.

Solar Thermal Energy

Solar thermal energy, sometimes called *concentrated solar power*, is one way to get energy from the sun. It doesn't directly create electricity. Instead, it uses the sun to create heat, which in turn runs a turbine to generate electricity.

One form of solar thermal power is called a *parabolic trough solar power plant*. In these power plants, curved or parabolic mirrors focus the heat of the sun onto a long, narrow tube. Inside the tube is some kind of liquid, such as synthetic oil. Sunlight, reflected from the mirrors onto the narrow tube, superheats the synthetic oil as it is pumped through the tube. Then, the tube flows through water, and the superheated oil instantly turns the water to steam. The steam runs a turbine, which generates electricity. The water cools the oil, which is pumped back to the mirrors, where it becomes superheated once again.

Parabolic trough power plants need a lot of open space and abundant sunlight. Desert areas are good places for these kinds of power plants. They use a lot of space, but not as much as coal mines and power plants.

Facing page: A parabolic trough solar power plant in California's Mojave Desert. Parabolic mirrors track the sun across the sky and focus the light on tubes containing synthetic oil. The oil becomes superheated, and is then used to boil water for steam turbine generators.

Another kind of solar thermal energy power plant is called a *power tower*. In this design, a tall tower holds some kind of liquid, like oil or liquid metal. Mirrors on the ground, called *heliostats*, reflect the sun's energy to the top of the tower. The liquid at the top of the tower becomes superheated. The liquid flows down the tower, through water, which generates steam. The steam runs a turbine that generates electricity.

Below: A solar power tower in Daggett, California.

The disadvantage of solar thermal energy power plants is that they are inefficient, producing smaller amounts of electricity than coal or nuclear power plants. The energy that power plants produce is measured in megawatts. One megawatt might power 400 to 800 homes, depending on the power usage of the home. Solar thermal plants usually average between 30 to 80 megawatts. An average coal power plant might average 600 megawatts or more. However, solar thermal power plants are clean. Their only waste product is steam.

Below: A California concentrated solar power plant.

Photovoltaic Energy

Solar thermal power plants make energy from the sun, but they work indirectly. They convert sunlight to heat, which makes steam, which powers a turbine, which generates electricity. By contrast, photovoltaic energy cells convert sunlight directly into electricity.

A photovoltaic cell is like a sandwich. Instead of bread, there is a metal plate on the bottom and a glass plate on top. Between the plates are two layers of silicon. Sunlight is composed of particles called photons. When a photon hits a silicon electron, it knocks the electron out of the atom. Those electrons are collected in electric wires.

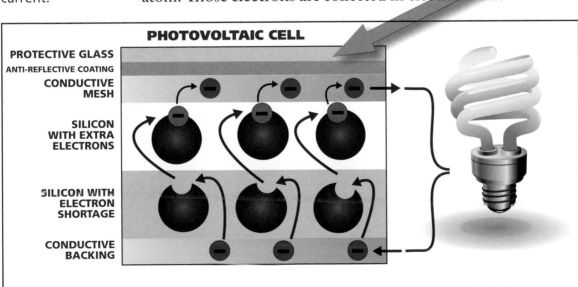

SUNLIGHT

PHOTOVOLTAIC CELL

PROTECTIVE GLASS
ANTI-REFLECTIVE COATING
CONDUCTIVE MESH

SILICON WITH EXTRA ELECTRONS

SILICON WITH ELECTRON SHORTAGE

CONDUCTIVE BACKING

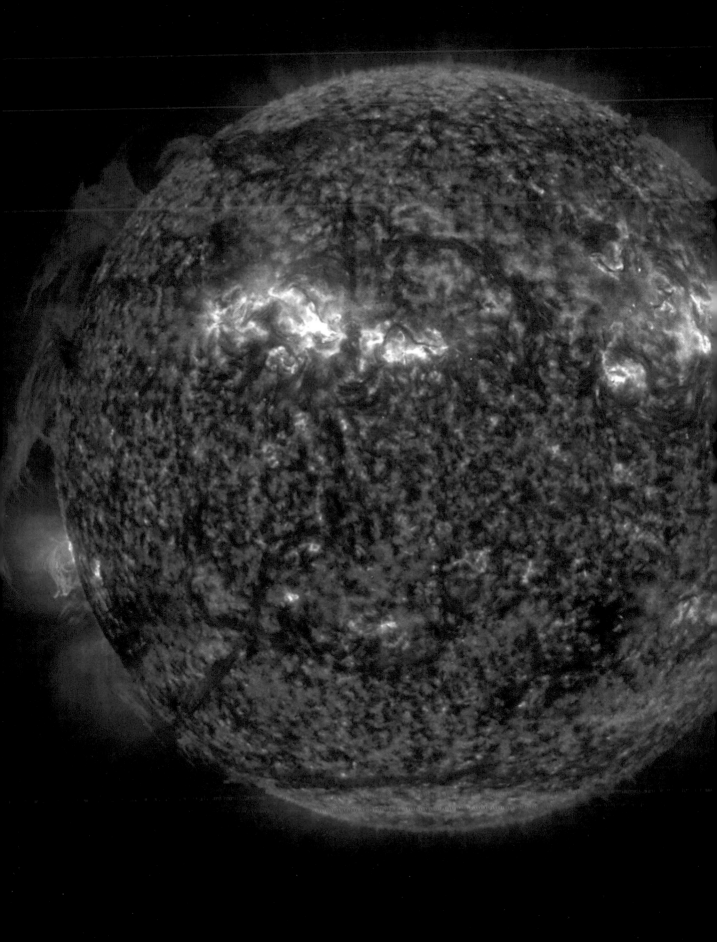

The electricity from a photovoltaic cell is in direct current—the same kind of electrical current that comes from a battery. In North America, our appliances all run on alternating current. So, the electricity from the photovoltaic cell has to be converted from direct to alternating current. This is done in an electrical box called an inverter. The inverter changes the charge from direct current to alternating current, which then can be used to give us the electricity we need.

Photovoltaic cells can be used in power plants. A large array of solar collectors feeds electricity to a central location, which is then distributed to places where it is needed. This is using solar power in the same way a community might use a coal-fired power plant. The electricity is generated in one location and distributed using a power grid.

Below: A silicon photovoltaic cell used on a satellite to convert sunlight directly into electricity.

Photovoltaic cell solar collectors can be put on rooftops, providing energy for single homes or businesses. If the solar collectors are large enough, and the building is fairly efficient, they might provide all of its electric needs.

In this decentralized model, solar collectors fill the needs of the home or business. If the home needs more electricity, they buy it from the local power plant. If the home has extra electricity, it is sold to the local power plant. Having the local power plant buy the extra electricity is called net metering. Many states have passed laws requiring power companies to buy back extra electricity.

In Germany, solar energy is very popular, partly because of net metering. People who invest in solar power collectors can actually get a check each month from the local utilities when they generate extra energy.

Below: A single family home with solar panels on its roof. In many states, power companies are required to purchase any extra energy generated by homes or businesses. This is called net metering. It encourages people to invest in renewable energy.

Solar Power Advantages

Perhaps the biggest advantage of solar power is that it is clean. No pollutants, chemicals, or waste is created when the cells make electricity. So, for every megawatt that is generated by solar energy, there is one less megawatt that needs to be generated by a fossil fuel plant. The less energy generated by fossil fuel power plants, the less pollution they create. This means that the more solar energy is generated, the less carbon dioxide and other pollutants are put into the air.

Another big advantage of solar power is that the power source is free. While oil must be drilled, and coal and uranium must be mined, the source for solar power is simply sunlight. And unlike fossil fuels, the costs of solar energy never rise.

Facing page: A maintenance worker at a solar energy farm.
Below: Sunlight is a free power source that is available to everyone.

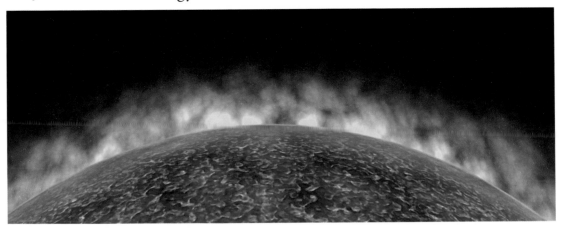

Many large cities have trouble meeting energy needs on hot, sunny, summer days. On the hottest days, people run their air conditioners, and that puts a huge drain on the power grid. Some cities have blackouts, where the energy produced can't keep up with the demand, so all the power goes out. Most cities, on very hot days, call businesses and ask them to voluntarily shut down, which prevents the blackouts. An advantage of solar power is that sunlight is most concentrated when the electric needs are greatest. Solar power is best when the needs are most intense, and so it can be used to prevent blackouts and shutdowns on the hottest days.

Solar power can work virtually anywhere. If a person builds a home far away from a city, and far away from electricity supplies, it might cost a lot of money to build a power line to get electricity to the home. But solar power can help provide that electricity. Solar cells can be put just about anywhere.

Right: A home with solar panels mounted on the roof. Solar power is a good energy alternative for remotely located homes that don't have access to a city's power grid.

Another advantage of solar energy is its safety. An enormous amount of time, money, and energy is put into keeping fossil fuel plants and nuclear plants safe. An oil spill can devastate the surrounding environment. Coal mine accidents often cause death or injury. The security companies and police SWAT teams that protect nuclear power plants must be alert to guard against terrorism.

By contrast, solar energy is safe from terrorist attacks. There is nothing in a solar energy plant that could devastate the environment. A breakdown in a solar energy plant might mean a broken mirror. A breakdown in a nuclear plant could mean a major disaster.

Below: Soldiers try to clean up the seashore covered with crude oil spilled from a tanker off the coast near Taean, South Korea, in 2007.

Solar Power Problems

Facing page:
A NASA image
showing a total
eclipse of the sun.
A big disadvantage
of solar energy, of
course, is that it
only works when
the sun is shining.
Scientists continue
to work on better
battery technology
so solar energy can
be stored and used
at night.

The most obvious problem of solar power is that it can only be generated when the sun is shining. No power can be generated at night, and only a little power can be generated on cloudy days. Scientists don't have any way to store electricity, except in batteries. Batteries are inefficient, and can contain dangerous chemicals. Until scientists invent a good way to store electricity, people using solar power will always have to rely on another energy source at night or when it is cloudy.

A big problem of photovoltaic cells is that they are still very expensive. Installing solar collectors on the roof of a home might cost 20 to 30 thousand dollars. Homeowners have to earn back that money over time. However, it might take 20 years or more.

Solar cell costs are falling rapidly. The more photovoltaic cells that are made, the more the prices drop. Many states now offer to pay part of the installation. State and federal governments have often offered tax breaks in an effort to make solar energy more affordable. However, the costs are still higher than most people can afford.

The first photovoltaic cells were built in the 1950s. Those cells had an efficiency of only 4 percent. That means that only 4 percent of the light that reached the cell was converted to electricity. Today, solar cells operate normally at about 15 to 20 percent. In laboratories, scientists have created solar cells that are more than 40 percent efficient. Technological developments could continue to push that efficiency even higher. However, higher efficiency usually means higher prices.

Another disadvantage is that many people dislike the look of solar panels. Instead of seeing grass and trees, they see solar cells. Instead of seeing rooftop shingles, people look at solar panels. Because they are large and often ugly, many people have rejected them for reasons of visual beauty. While coal-fired power plants are ugly too, these power plants can usually be hidden from public view. Solar panels cannot always be hidden.

One way to "hide" solar power collectors is in shingles. Already on the market, solar shingles look and function like regular home shingles, but they also are solar power collectors. While these solar shingles are very expensive, the price will likely drop as they become more common.

Below: Solar panels attached to roof shingles create energy during a test in Golden, Colorado.

Increasing the Use of Solar Power

Several things need to be in place to create a shift toward solar power. First, government funding is critical. State and federal policies can help lower prices for the purchase and installation of solar power collectors. Tax credits can help offset the high startup costs of solar energy projects.

Laws must be passed that will force local utilities to buy back extra power, the process called net metering. This may also require updating the country's antiquated electrical power grid.

States and communities need to enter into business deals to buy huge amounts of solar collectors. This will bring the cost of solar collectors down, and encourage widespread use.

For example, communities could require all new homes to use solar shingles. The higher costs could be offset by the states and communities that would benefit in the long term.

People need to be educated about the problems with burning fossil fuels, and how solar energy is part of the solution. Awareness of the problem and solution is necessary for action.

Finally, we have to leave our municipal model of energy—the idea that one power plant in each city will create enough energy for all the city's needs. We need to move to a distributed model, where every home can generate some electricity, and then draw on a central power plant if they need extra electricity.

Below: The U.S. Capitol building in Washington, D.C. By passing policies and increasing funding, lawmakers could help solar energy grow.

The Future of Solar Power

Today, solar energy makes up only one-tenth of one percent of electricity in the United States. But exciting new discoveries and inventions are creating a bright future for solar power.

Research is ongoing to create a solar paint. People could put this paint on their houses, and the paint itself would collect solar energy. Imagine if every building in North America was painted with this, it could make every building a solar collector.

Some scientists are exploring whether roads could be embedded with photovoltaic cells. As the sun shines, roads become solar collectors. Other inventors have proposed building floating photovoltaic cells and setting them up as artificial islands in the ocean.

Australian engineers have created a window that can be put on buildings, which acts as a solar collector. Scientists are working on a low-cost plastic photovoltaic cell, overcoming the initial high price of the solar collector. Researchers are continuing to perfect the solar powered shingle, which if put on all new houses could revolutionize energy in North America.

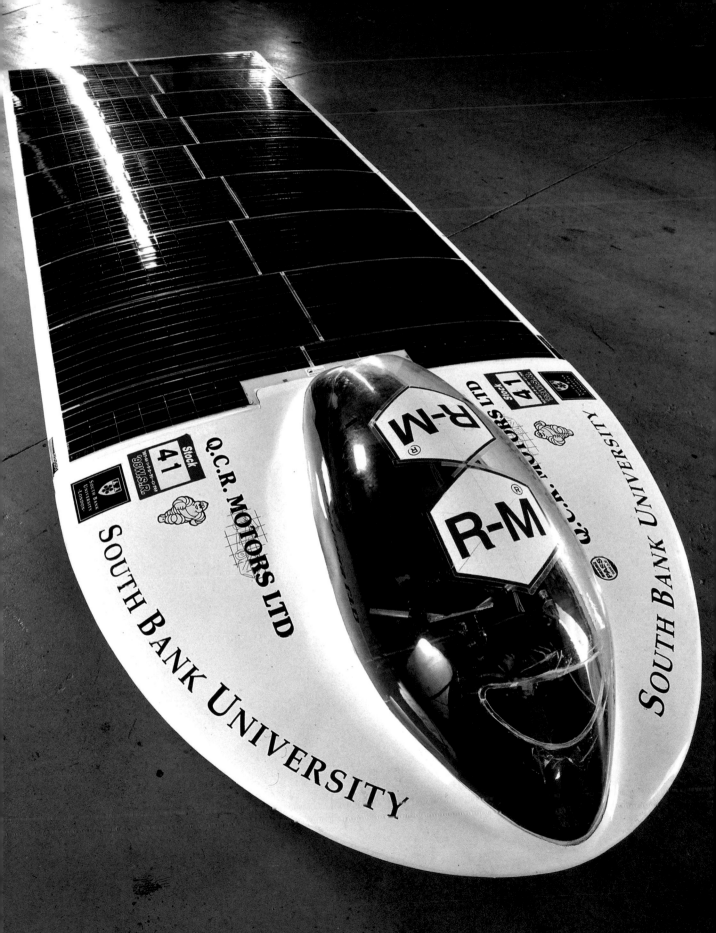

Solar scientists are working to create new kinds of solar collectors that make use of all the spectrums of light, not just the visible light that we see. The efficiency of solar power cells has been constantly improving.

Some critics say we should wait, that solar power is still too inefficient, and photovoltaic cells are still too expensive. The problem with waiting is that the more solar power that is installed, the more solar scientists learn. The more solar collectors that are installed, the cheaper the price becomes. With a world in crisis, solar power can no longer wait.

Can solar power become our main source of electricity? A lot depends on the combined efforts of scientists, economists, and citizens who demand an efficient, renewable source of energy.

The move toward solar power also depends on leadership. The world needs leaders who are willing to move away from fossil fuels. Leadership can help organize a world that uses less fossil fuels, and more solar power and other renewables.

Below: It's only a matter of time before solar power becomes a cheaper and more efficient energy source.

Glossary

CARBON DIOXIDE

Normally a gas, carbon dioxide is a chemical compound made up of two oxygen atoms and one carbon atom. Its chemical symbol is CO_2. Carbon dioxide in the earth's atmosphere acts as a greenhouse gas.

FOSSIL FUEL

Fuels that are created by the remains of ancient plants and animals that were buried and then subjected to millions of years of heat, pressure, and bacteria. Oil and coal are the most common fossil fuels burned to create electricity. Natural gas is also a fossil fuel. Burning fossil fuels releases carbon dioxide into the atmosphere, contributing to global warming.

GREENHOUSE EFFECT

The earth naturally warms because of the greenhouse effect. The surface of the earth absorbs some solar radiation, and reflects some. The reflected rays either pass back into space, or are absorbed and reflected back by gasses in the earth's atmosphere. Carbon dioxide is a major greenhouse gas that is produced by burning fossil fuels. When too much solar radiation is absorbed, the earth warms up, which alters climates around the world.

GREENHOUSE GAS

Any gas that is good at absorbing and retaining the sun's heat. Carbon dioxide, which is released into the atmosphere by the burning of fossil fuels, is a greenhouse gas. Greenhouse gasses contribute to a gradual warming of the earth, which is called the greenhouse effect.

INVERTER

An electrical box used to convert direct current (DC) that comes from solar panels into alternating current (AC). Electrical devices in North America use AC current.

NET METERING

When an electric utility buys back electricity from a home solar power collector that the home doesn't need.

PHOTOVOLTAIC CELL

A device that generates electricity directly from the light of the sun.

POWER GRID

Power lines, transformers, transmission substations, and all of the parts of the system that bring electricity from a power plant into people's homes.

POWER TOWER

A type of solar thermal power plant. Mirrors reflect the energy of the sun to the top of a tower, where liquid becomes superheated. The liquid is used to create steam, which turns turbines to create electricity.

RENEWABLE ENERGY

Any kind of energy where the source won't get used up. Solar power, waterpower, and wind power are examples of renewable energy.

SOLAR THERMAL ENERGY

Electricity generated by using the heat of the sun. Large mirrors intensify the energy of the sun, superheating a liquid that will then turn water into steam. The steam runs a turbine that generates electricity.

Index

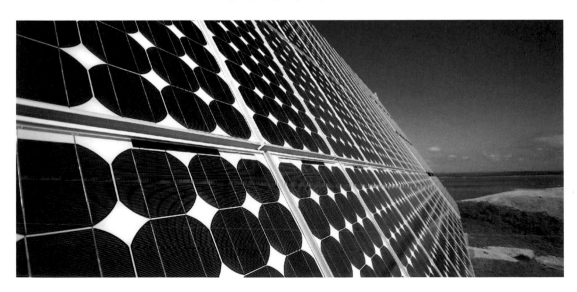